Dedicated with love
to my sons:
Collin, Jude, Spencer, and Rex

May the Lord be your confidence
and keep your foot from being caught.
May you fear him and walk in his ways
all the days of your life.

IDENTITY

31-DAY DEVOTIONALS
FOR TEENAGERS

A Series

CHELSEA KINGSTON ERICKSON
Series Editor

Anxiety: Finding the Better Story, by Liz Edrington
Identity: Discovering Who You Are in Christ, by Lindsey Carlson

IDENTITY

Discovering Who You Are in Christ

LINDSEY CARLSON

P&R
PUBLISHING
P.O. BOX 817 • PHILLIPSBURG • NEW JERSEY 08865-0817

Cover design by Jelena Mirkovic

Printed in the United States of America

Library of Congress Cataloging-in-Publication Data

Names: Carlson, Lindsey, 1982- author.
Title: Identity : discovering who you are in Christ / Lindsey Carlson.
Description: Phillipsburg, New Jersey : P&R Publishing Company, [2024] | Series: 31-day devotionals for teenagers | Includes bibliographical references. | Summary: "Who are you? You're probably trying to figure that out! If you're feeling overwhelmed, use this devotional to fix your identity on an unshakable foundation and live with Christ-centered confidence"-- Provided by publisher.
Identifiers: LCCN 2023058294 | ISBN 9798887790244 (paperback) | ISBN 9798887790251 (epub)
Subjects: LCSH: Confidence--Religious aspects--Christianity. | Identity (Philosophical concept)--Religious aspects--Christianity.
Classification: LCC BV4647.C63 C37 2024 | DDC 111/.82--dc23/eng/20240222
LC record available at https://lccn.loc.gov/2023058294

CONTENTS

HOW DOES WHO I AM IMPACT HOW I LIVE?

WHO DOES GOD SAY THAT I AM?

Who am I?

As a teenager, I attempted to define myself by my great hair, my flowered Dr. Martens, and my stellar sense of humor. I tended to base my sense of self-worth on the externals. What I saw in the mirror—how my hair looked, how straight my teeth were, and how much weight I'd gained or lost—regularly dictated whether I felt loved or accepted. But really, how we look isn't who we are, and it should never determine whether or not we feel loved.

Sometimes we describe who we are by pointing to our relationships. Someone at my church might say, "Oh, that's Lindsey Carlson. She's Collin's mom and the pastor's wife." But though you may love your family and friends, they don't define *who* you are.

What makes you *you*? Where do you find your identity or your sense of belonging? What values or factors guide you as you consider who you are? Maybe it's not your looks or your sense of humor that make you feel special. Maybe it's your performance at school or your extracurricular activities. Do you want to be known by others as smart, talented, or impressive? Why?

We live in a culture that's obsessed with knowing and finding yourself. We're taught to "be true to you." We identify with people who are like us. We start groups and clubs. We love to "find our people" and "discover our tribe."

But when we seek our identity in the people who "get us," we may fail to find understanding from the God who made us. To truly know ourselves, to identify our purpose, and to flourish within a community who loves and accepts us, we must discover the identity *God* gives us.

Merriam-Webster defines *identity* as "the distinguishing character or personality of an individual." And what distinguishes a Christian? They have professed faith in Christ, and they are in the process of becoming more and more like Jesus.

We all belong to God because he made us. As our Creator and Ruler, he commands us to obey all his laws perfectly, all the time. But we don't. Our hearts are filled with thoughts and desires that don't please God. We sin. We can't fake perfection or become perfect through hard work. We can't measure up to God's standard or reflect his righteous character.

We often try to ignore or lower God's standards, but whether we like it or not, God will judge all humanity according to his perfect standard. When he does, only one person will measure up. And we must identify with him.

Jesus Christ came to earth to *identify with us.*

Jesus came to earth to humbly do his Father's will. He was tempted in every way and never sinned (Hebrews 4:15). He lived the life we couldn't live—one of perfect obedience—so that, through faith, we could exchange our wretchedness for his robes of righteousness. We find our identity in his life.

Instead of punishing us for our sins, God punished Jesus in our place. When God's wrath against sin was poured out on Jesus at the cross, we exchanged our punishment for everlasting life. We find our identity in his death.

Three days after Jesus's body was buried and sealed in a tomb, God raised him back to life and conquered death forever. Because Jesus lives, we too will be raised to a new and better life, when we trust in Jesus. We find our identity in his resurrection.

Romans 10:9 says, "If you confess with your mouth that Jesus is Lord and believe in your heart that God raised him from the dead, you will be saved." God grants sinners like you and me a new identity. Because Christ lived, died, and was raised to new life, you can die to sin, be made like Christ, and be raised to live with him forever. When you come to him by grace, through faith, you take on the identity of Christ. You are chosen, beloved, and redeemed. Now you are distinguished by Christlikeness.

Friend, do you believe that Jesus is Lord? Have you ever acknowledged that out loud?

When the grace of God appeared through Christ, God made a way for you to be what you could not be on your own—a beloved son or daughter. You no longer have to work to earn God's love or acceptance. You are loved by God (1 Thessalonians 1:4), chosen by grace (Romans 11:5), holy and beloved (Colossians 3:12), rich in faith (James 2:5), and part of "a royal priesthood, a holy nation, a people for his own possession" (1 Peter 2:9). This is who you are, *in Christ*.

Puritan pastor Robert Murray M'Cheyne wrote, "For every look at yourself, take ten looks at Christ." When you wonder who you are, look to the life, death, and resurrection of Christ and gain *his* valuable perspective. Looking to Jesus helps you discover who you are. You have the privilege of being identified with him and made like him! Fix your eyes on Jesus, for he is your steadfast, unwavering source of acceptance and love.

This book is broken down into three sections that will help you discover who you are on your own and who God says you are now that you are in Christ. By looking to Scripture and considering the life and character of Jesus, we will explore three essential identity questions:

- Who does God say that I am?
- What is my purpose?
- How does who I am impact how I live?

It is my prayer that through these readings, you might discover who you are in Christ, find a biblical sense of purpose, and then entrust yourself to the work of God's Spirit in and through you. I want you to know what it means to "find your identity in Christ," so that you can begin to rest in who he is. The gospel frees you to live with your confidence and joy in Jesus.

Friend, God already knows who you are. Do you? No sin or struggle with identity is big enough to keep you from the boundless love of God. Come to Jesus and ask him to show you who *he is*. He will forgive you, heal you, and make you more like himself. Let him help you discover who you are.

WHO AM I?

Who are you?

In this first section, you will discover who God says that you are, if you are in Christ Jesus.

As a child of the living God, you had value long before you drew your first breath. But as a forgiven, loved, and redeemed son or daughter of God through the work of Jesus, you now have every reason to live fully satisfied with who you are, because your identity is rooted in your relationship with Christ.

In the next ten daily readings, we'll discover ten ways God grants a secure identity to those who place their faith in Jesus.

Day 1

I AM CREATED AND KNOWN

*God created man in his own image, in the image of
God he created him; male and female he created
them. And God blessed them. (Genesis 1:27–28)*

Lily loved houseplants. After working at a plant nursery over the
summer, she'd spent nearly all the money she earned to buy plants
of every shape and size.

Lily learned the scientific names of each plant but gave affec-
tionate pet names to every spider plant, snake plant, fern, and
flowing English ivy. She used an app to diagnose diseases in their
leaves and to remind her to fertilize the soil. She made watering
schedules to ensure that each plant had proper moisture. She carefully rotated each plant baby throughout her bedroom, moving
them from corners to windowsills, so that they could enjoy the
appropriate amount of sunlight or shade needed to grow and thrive.

Have you ever wondered if anyone cares this much about you?
Or wondered what you'd have to do to gain or hold on to this kind
of attention? Do you long to be fully known? Guess what? You are
already loved and cared for. You are *precious to God.*

God created mankind in his image. You belong to him. He
designed you and gave you life. He didn't have to develop an
interest in you or learn how to care for you; he's always had a
plan. Our triune God—Father, Son, and Holy Spirit—tells us
right from the beginning of the Bible why he created us. "God
said, 'Let us make [mankind] in our image, after our likeness'"
(Genesis 1:26). God created you beautifully in his image so that
you would reflect *who he is.*

God will till the hard soil of your heart and nourish you so that
you will become more like Jesus. This isn't about how you look on
the outside. Scripture teaches that Jesus didn't look special; he had
"no beauty that we should desire him" (Isaiah 53:2). He was born

into a carpenter's family. His brothers' reputations could have poked holes in his kingly credibility. God accomplished all his purposes through Christ, despite how Jesus looked to the world. God knows exactly what you need to grow and flourish under his care so that your life will become a beautiful testimony.

When others look at your life, God wants *his nature* to show. As God cares for you, you mature in the faith and thrive under his provision. Less of you, more of him. No matter how it may seem, his attention never drifts away from you. Just as God cares for the flowers of the field, he always provides for you (Matthew 6:25–34). The light of Christ's presence always shines on you. His Spirit always waters you with his Word. Your Father knows when to shield you from the scorching sun and when to send rains in their season. He will shower you with his goodness.

Your heavenly Father knows you personally. You belong to him. He created you, he built you to reflect his character, and he called you by name in order to bless you and to set specific good works of grace before you.

Embrace who you are. You are created by God and made like him.

Ask: When has insecurity led you to believe that you are unseen, uncared for, or unloved? Can you think of any obvious ways in which God has cared for you or demonstrated his love?

Confess: Lord, I often fear that I am too _____ to be worthy of your love. Forgive me for wrongly believing that my life is meaningless unless I make something of myself. Help me to understand who you are and how you created me to be like Jesus, so that the world would see your love.

Discover: In Christ, I am created and known by God, in order to reflect the beauty of the gospel.

I AM A SOUGHT-OUT SINNER

*But the LORD God called to the man and said
to him, "Where are you?" (Genesis 3:9)*

As a teenager, I committed an act of petty crime that I regret decades later.

One afternoon, my friends and I went to the mall to try on clothes. In the dressing room, I slipped on a pair of plaid pajama pants with a Mickey Mouse patch on the back pocket. They were cute—but not $18.99 cute. Before I could return them to their hanger, my friend reached over, grabbed the pants out of my hands, and shoved them in a bag beneath the clothes she'd already paid for. "Just take them," she urged me.

I knew shoplifting was wrong. But as horrified as I was by her suggestion, I did not protest. Instead, I walked silently out of the store without paying, feeling sick.

Back at my house, my friend victoriously thrust the pants in my direction. I sheepishly tore off the tags and put them on. When my mother asked about my "purchase," I panicked and lied, hiding that I'd picked up a new label too—*shoplifter*. That night, I attempted to bury my guilt and the pajama pants deep in a dresser drawer.

Thankfully, hiding didn't work.

In Genesis 3, we read the story of how the first man and woman, Adam and Eve, rejected God's plan for their identity. God had given them a good world to enjoy, but they disobeyed him. The Bible calls this rebellion against God *sin*, and every human being has followed in Adam and Eve's footsteps. We are all sinners.

After Adam and Eve sinned, they hid. But God called to Adam in the garden, asking, "Where are you?" Through conviction and repentance, he calls to you too. Where are you?

What humiliating labels are you attempting to hide? Will you respond to God when he calls you out of the darkness?

God searches for sinners because he loves us. He knows the depths of our shame. And out of his generosity, he sent Jesus to preach peace to those who were far off and to those who were near (Ephesians 2:17). When we trust in Jesus, God removes our guilt and gives us a new label—*forgiven*.

Christ sought me out when I was a shoplifter. Today I'm forgiven. Instead of God's enemy, now I'm his friend. Instead of a rebel, I'm forever his beloved child. Christ never stumbles blindly into your brokenness; he enters willingly. He takes on the ugliest of offenses. You don't have to pretend that you're someone you're not. God fully understands the sinful depths of *your* heart. He knows *your* need for rescue.

Sinner, you are sought out by Christ. Stop hiding. Come to him. Believe and confess. Jesus will dress you in his righteousness. He will strip away every shameful label and gloriously clothe you in forgiveness and freedom.

Ask: What shameful label(s) do you need Christ to remove? Are there areas of sin in your life that you wish God couldn't see? How does it feel to consider that God already knows the full story?

Confess: Lord, I am tempted to hide my sinful thoughts, desires, and actions from you. I foolishly believe that they remain hidden from your sight. Help me to be honest about my failings—both to myself and to you—so that I might hide myself in the gospel of my salvation, given to me through Christ while I was still his enemy.

Discover: In Christ, I am sought out in my sin, so that I can be forgiven by God and freed from my shame.

I AM A COVENANT RECIPIENT

*He is the mediator of a new covenant, so that those
who are called may receive the promised eternal
inheritance, since a death has occurred that redeems
them from [their] transgressions. (Hebrews 9:15)*

Have you ever made a deal with your parents? Maybe you agree that if you wash the dishes every day, they'll give you a little extra spending money for summer camp. Ideally, in this arrangement both you and your parents profit. In Scripture, God makes similar (but far more serious) arrangements with his people that are called covenants. A covenant is a relational agreement between two parties who promise to work together for each other's good. In the ancient world, two nations, groups, or individuals might enter a covenant for their own protection or security.

In the Bible, God—who is all powerful and needs nothing —generously enters into covenants with mankind, in order to do good to those who follow and obey him. Throughout the Old Testament, God routinely made and kept promises that displayed his perfect covenant-keeping faithfulness to his unfaithful people.

Humans are all promise-breakers. This could lead us to question whether God will keep his promises to us. In Deuteronomy 28:2, we read, "All these blessings shall come upon you and overtake you, *if* you obey the voice of the Lord your God." It's easy to stumble over that little word *if*. What happens when your actions don't line up with God's expectations? Will God bless you *if* you don't make time to read your Bible? *If* you forget to pray? *If* you struggle to forgive others?

We have a big problem: our sins aren't a matter of "if" but "when." We're like students who want good grades but don't want to study. Even if we want to love and obey God, it is easier to follow our hearts into doing what we want. We are natural covenant-breakers. Good thing we have the good news of the gospel.

Christ is the solution to our sin and our faithlessness. Specifically, Hebrews 9:15 assures us that Jesus is the "mediator of a new covenant." God fulfilled all the old covenants through Jesus, the only covenant-keeper, who could perfectly satisfy all the "ifs" we failed to fulfill. And now, we await the day when God's final covenant will be fulfilled and Jesus will share all the blessings of his inheritance with us—his undeserving brothers and sisters.

First John 3:1 says, "See what kind of love the Father has given to us, that we should be called children of God; and so we are." We come to Christ as forgiven children, eager to receive good from our Father. We have a new identity that we didn't work to earn! We are no longer wicked children awaiting God's judgment and punishment. Now, we are beloved sons and daughters awaiting our full inheritance.

When you believe and confess that Jesus died to purchase your forgiveness, God no longer identifies you by your sin (Hebrews 10:16–17). Christ's reward becomes yours, even though you can't fully uphold his commands.

If you trust in the Son of God and look to him for salvation, *then* Christ is your confidence, and his inheritance is your reward. Through Christ, you are no longer a covenant-breaker—you are a covenant-keeping inheritor!

Ask: What do you assume God requires you to do before he'll keep his promises to you? What blessings do you fear God will withhold from you when you break his commands?

Confess: Lord, I confess that I often attempt to impress you by keeping your law by my own strength. I foolishly want my behavior to be the reason you bless me. Forgive me, O Lord, when I forget that you have given me a better covenant of grace. Help me to trust the work of Christ on my behalf.

Discover: In Christ, because of his perfect work, I am a confident recipient of the covenant promises of God.

I AM A CHILD OF PROMISE

*This means that it is not the children of the flesh
who are the children of God, but the children of the
promise are counted as offspring. (Romans 9:8)*

It was a sunny morning in Mrs. Farrar's youth discipleship class. Although I don't remember the lesson or the theme verse, I remember her concluding statement: "Just like standing in a garage doesn't mean you're a car, attending church doesn't mean you're a Christian."

Wait. What? I'd never considered that some of the teenagers sitting beside me might not be Christians. Imagine my shock when I realized—years later—that I wasn't one myself! I knew Jesus as a Bible character, but I didn't understand that he'd died to reconcile me to God.

Even though I was in the church building whenever the doors opened, I didn't understand the gospel. Each week, I listened to sermons under a gigantic stained glass window of Jesus. Though he had holes in his hands, I didn't understand how Christ was any different than David, Moses, or Jonah. I was a child of the church, but I wasn't a child of the promise.

Romans 9:8 warns that salvation and eternal reward aren't guaranteed by being born into the "right" family. To be a true child of God and a recipient of his promised inheritance, each and every person must become a child of the promise by professing faith in Jesus. Today, God's children can be found in every nation. Through Christ, God made a way for men and women of every ethnicity to be welcomed into the family of God.

On our own, we're spiritually lost—we're born with a hard heart, and we depend on God for the hope of salvation. You can't earn your way into the family with your good behavior. You can't argue your way into receiving God's inheritance. Romans 9:16 explains that your adoption into God's family "depends not on human will or exertion, but on God, who has mercy." God kindly calls you to himself, by his grace. When you believe and profess faith in Jesus, God makes you a part of his family.

God searches for those who are lost! He will pursue you in order to fulfill all his promises to you. The Father promises good to his children: new hearts, redemption, his continual presence, his help, his strength, and his comfort. Are you his child? Are his promises yours?

A church-kid exterior may trick your parents or your youth director, but it earns you nothing. An ability to spout Bible trivia won't save you. To become God's child and enjoy your Father's promises, your heart must be transformed by his grace.

Be honest with yourself about the source of your faith. Maybe you are placing your hope of salvation in what you know or where you are on Sunday morning. Or perhaps you are deeply aware of your sin and convinced of your need for God's forgiveness. If you have chosen to trust in his resurrected Son as your only hope of salvation, then he has changed who you are. Instead of a rebellious child, you are now a child of God, through Christ. All his promises are yours.

> **Ask:** Have you ever assumed that God is pleased with you, based solely on your church attendance? How else are you tempted to prove yourself?
>
> **Confess:** Lord, I confess that it's easy to live on autopilot, never questioning where I misunderstand your Word and your ways. I need your help to see myself clearly and to understand when I've failed to depend on your mercy. Help me place my trust in you.
>
> **Discover:** In Christ, I am a child of the promise, included in the family of God by the grace of God.

I AM CHOSEN AND BELOVED

For you are a people holy to the LORD your God. The LORD your God has chosen you to be a people for his treasured possession, out of all the peoples who are on the face of the earth. (Deuteronomy 7:6)

Leah learned to play the piano by watching videos online. A friend forwarded her a reel of a girl about her age who was teaching her viewers how to play a pop singer's latest single. Leah watched the reel repeatedly, practicing as she went. Then she took a deep dive into the piano player's profile, scrolling through all her tutorials and eagerly waiting for new posts.

It wasn't the content-creator's piano concerts that hooked Leah; it was how she connected to her favorite influencer. By following her channel, she gained a front-row seat to her life: she met her family and friends, she saw inside her home, she heard hilarious stories, and she watched how she dressed.

Despite her fangirl loyalty, though, Leah remained a faceless number to the influencer on the other side of the screen—who measured her followers' worth in clicks, views, and purchases. Have you ever followed someone online whom you feel like you know but who doesn't even know you exist? It's strange to think about how connected you can feel to an influencer—even caring about them and the details of their life—while knowing that their feelings aren't mutual. Why do we love to follow people who don't know our name and who couldn't pick us out of a crowd? Sadly, we sometimes imagine that God is similarly distant and disconnected. He isn't.

God—the Sovereign Lord, who rules and reigns on high—is interested and invested in our lives. He does not view his people as small and insignificant followers. Indeed, his interest in us is far more personal.

In today's verse, God the Creator addresses his followers (the nation of Israel), whom he has the right to command, in a way that relationally connects his people to his covenant love. God directs Israel's attention and obedience by declaring that they are holy to him and that they are his *treasured* possession.

Now that Christ has come, God has made a way for all sinners to personally connect with Jesus and enjoy his covenant love forever. By grace, through faith, passive *viewers* of God are transformed into *faithful followers of Jesus* who are "chosen and precious" in the sight of God (1 Peter 2:4).

Your life is significant to God. You are not a nameless face or an insignificant observer—rather, you are called to be holy, you are God's chosen and treasured possession, and you are an active participant in God's family.

God is no ordinary content creator or influencer. He knows you, and he cares about you, long after you begin to trust in him. He will grant you true significance that only comes from following Jesus. As his child, you are invited to enjoy his creation and to influence others with his love.

Ask: God knows and cares about you in a personal way—how does this change your perspective? How might you actively learn from Jesus by knowing and caring about *him* more?

Confess: Father, I confess that sometimes I think of you as someone "out there," someone far away and uninvolved in my life. Forgive me for prioritizing so many other things over entering into and enjoying your presence. Help me know you and love you more than fame or wealth.

Discover: In Christ, I am chosen and beloved by God.

I AM A FRIEND OF GOD

And the Scripture was fulfilled that says, "Abraham believed God, and it was counted to him as righteousness" —and he was called a friend of God. (James 2:23)

Have you ever had to sit alone at a lunch table? Or been excluded from an outing with a friend group? Maybe, at the end of a terrible day, you've felt desperate for comforting words from a friend, but you had no one to text. When we're lonely, it's easy for us to feel overlooked, misunderstood, and unworthy of friendship.

Because God has designed us to flourish in our friendships, experiences with fair-weather friends are even more painful. Sometimes our friends lie to us, gossip about us, betray us, or abandon us. When we inevitably disappoint, offend, or sin against them, we are tempted to ghost or give up on one another rather than working to reconcile.

When we've been burned by other people, we learn to fear friendship. We may begin to believe that no one likes us, or we may worry that something about us repels good friends.

But did you know that God often uses seasons of loneliness and friendships with broken people to encourage us to become more secure in *his* friendship? When "Abraham believed God . . . it was counted to him as righteousness," and "he was called a friend of God." Belief begins our friendship with God. When we are lonely, God wants us to come to him in prayer, confessing all our feelings, desires, and needs and trusting that he will draw near and listen as a friend.

As we wait on him, he generously provides wisdom and help, always according to his perfect timing. We learn to trust him, even if we don't understand all his ways. We realize that God hears our prayers and delights to help us—because he is a true friend.

The news of God's friendship should affirm and comfort you when you feel lonely, hurt, or unloved! When you were dead in your sin and trespasses and unworthy of friendship, the God of the universe took on flesh to befriend you. You were once God's enemy. But now, through Jesus, you are forever identified as God's friend.

God does not expect you to earn his friendship; you already have it. You are God's friend, through Christ, because of his covenant promises, granted to you because you are a chosen and beloved child of the faith.

When you betray God, he repeatedly forgives you. When your communication is lacking, he never assumes the worst about you, and he never withholds his help. Jesus is your friend—he sticks closer than a brother at all times because he loves you.

Ask: Knowing that you have Christ's enduring friendship, how ought you to interact with others?

Confess: Lord, I often desire friendships with people more than I desire friendship with you. Forgive me for failing to come to you for your perfect companionship and love. Help me to rest in knowing that you will never leave me or forsake me.

Discover: In Christ, I am a friend of God.

I AM HELD AND HELPED

If the Lord had not been my help, my soul would soon have lived in the land of silence. When I thought, "My foot slips," your steadfast love, O Lord, held me up. (Psalm 94:17–18)

No one in Ben's family knew that he'd been keeping a dark secret for the past three years. He was addicted to pornography, and he was too ashamed to ask for help.

One Sunday morning at church, the pastor preached about Jesus's healing of a paralyzed man. Before restoring the man's physical health and enabling him to rise and walk, Jesus assured him that his sins were forgiven. Ben's pastor explained that when we feel paralyzed by sin and weighed down by shame, we need the good news of the gospel in order to rise and walk. Something changed in Ben's heart.

The Holy Spirit granted Ben a glimpse of hope. Even though he still felt embarrassed by his addiction to pornography, he realized the gospel meant that God's forgiveness was already his because of what Jesus had done for him. Through the Holy Spirit, Ben found the confidence he needed to stand up and walk away from his sin and shame.

Later than day, Ben asked his dad if they could go for a drive and talk privately. Reminded of God's grace in Jesus, Ben uncomfortably unloaded the details of his entanglement with porn. His father listened, grieved with him, and then confessed that he too had once battled a pornography addiction but that, in God's kindness, he had found forgiveness and healing. Ben's dad extended him grace as he reassured him of God's love and forgiveness, along with his own. He then offered to help him strategize ways to fight temptation.

Have you ever stumbled into a sin pattern that felt too enormous or embarrassing to confess? If you do in the future, do you know who you might talk to? You may not have a parent who would respond like Ben's dad, but you do have a gracious and trustworthy audience with the Holy Spirit. When you turn to God in repentance, he will draw near to you and help.

In today's passage, the psalmist confidently declares that it's God's steadfast love that holds him up. Not the psalmist's resolve. Not the psalmist's confidence. God's love held him up. If you've trusted in Christ, you are held and helped when you feel lost, broken, or helpless in the face of sin. In Christ, your help is near.

In addition to hearing us personally, God also gives us his people, the church, to help us when we are tempted. I encourage you to find an older Christian you could talk to about your own struggle with sin—whether a parent, pastor, youth leader, or teacher.

Heed the Lord's call to come to him for help. Cry out to him. Now is the right time. The Spirit is listening—Christ is your help.

Ask: Who do you turn to for help? When you fall into sinful habits, what prevents you from quickly going to the Lord and asking for help?

Confess: Lord, forgive me for the times when I pridefully believe that I can solve all my problems. I cannot correct my own wayward heart or keep my foot from stumbling into sin. Help me to believe that you will hold me, help me, and provide me with good.

Discover: In Christ, I am held by God and helped by the Holy Spirit.

I AM CHALLENGED AND CHANGED

Those sanctified in Christ Jesus [are] called to be saints together with all those who in every place call upon the name of our Lord Jesus Christ. (1 Corinthians 1:2)

Isn't it exciting to learn something new? Think of a time when you learned a new dance or tried a viral internet challenge. Maybe you picked up a new sport or downloaded an app that would teach you a new language. Was it fun at the beginning? What about later on? So often, growing in a skill is hard. The growth process challenges and changes us.

Understanding new concepts takes time and practice. To play an instrument skillfully, you must practice for many hours before you see noteworthy progress. And if you've never run a mile in your life, those mid-run chest pains will likely make you think you're dying at first. When learning takes more time and effort than we expect, we can grow discouraged, and we may be tempted to give up entirely. We want success without putting in the work to refine our abilities.

Have you ever felt the same way about following Jesus? Perhaps you're excited about your faith, but you keep struggling with the same old sin. Perhaps you doubt what you hear and read about God. These are normal struggles.

You don't need to panic or give up. In the Christian life, growth pains are a sign that the Holy Spirit is at work! He is purifying you, refining you, and making you new—so you will look more and more like Jesus. This process can be painful, but the change it produces is worth it.

In 1 Corinthians 1:2, the apostle Paul writes to "those sanctified in Christ Jesus." To be sanctified means to be set apart for holy service to God. Paul reminds Christians that being sanctified is part of our new identity.

Scripture teaches that you, as a follower of Jesus, are both justified and sanctified. When you believe and profess faith in God, he instantly makes you right with him (that's what it means to be justified). And as the Spirit works in your heart, you will also grow in faith and maturity (that's what it means to be sanctified). As long as you're living on this earth, God will work to refine you and make you more like Jesus.

The Lord knows how to shape you into his image; the pressure is off your shoulders. Although you do need to practice your faith, ultimately you are not responsible for figuring out how to grow in maturity. God is more committed and invested in your spiritual growth than you could ever be! As you look to him, he will direct your steps and teach you how to walk in his ways.

God uses everything—your interests, gifts, talents, abilities, and opportunities—to sanctify you. You are a work in progress. Even when the process is a challenge, trust that God is changing you into the person he's designed you to become.

Ask: Are you tempted to worry when spiritual growth feels too difficult or painful? Do you attempt to find your confidence in how quickly your faith is growing?

Confess: I confess, Lord, that I often want to take control of my life. Forgive me for trying to be complete and perfect apart from you. Help me to trust that only you can perfectly see all my weaknesses, faults, and sins and that only you can lovingly restore me. Help me to value what you value, Lord. May I become more and more like Jesus.

Discover: In Christ, I am pressed and purified in order to become more like Jesus.

I AM A COMFORTED SUFFERER

Blessed be the God and Father of our Lord Jesus Christ,
the Father of mercies and God of all comfort, who
comforts us in all our affliction. (2 Corinthians 1:3–4)

Each day Randall sat alone at the lunch table. He'd been in high school for six months now, and he hadn't made a single friend. He'd assumed that, as a freshman, he'd meet a group of guys who he would enjoy hanging out with. Instead, it seemed that everyone had found their friend groups and that he'd been excluded.

Randall wondered if he was the problem. Was he too weird? Or annoying? Or too much of a nerd? He felt like such a loser. Sometimes he fantasized about what might help him fit in. A lot of kids cursed, trash-talked teachers, and teased one another. Maybe if he joked around more or bought new clothes, then people would like him. Randall's sense of identity was shaken.

Have you ever felt this way? Perhaps you've struggled to connect with people recently. Loneliness is a form of suffering that often prompts insecurity. In times of loneliness, believers can find security in the comfort of God.

In today's verse, Paul praises God, calling him the "Father of mercies and God of all comfort" because of his proven ability to comfort his people in every affliction. We see God's provision most clearly through his only begotten Son, Jesus, who is familiar with our grief and able to carry all of our sorrows. Jesus experienced the brokenness of this world firsthand. He suffered loneliness, pain, and affliction. He's "been there, done that," and he has compassion for you. When no one gets you, Jesus does.

Jesus turned to the Father for comfort and help amid his suffering. In the garden of Gethsemane, the night he was arrested, Jesus stepped away from his disciples to be alone with God and pray. He asked his friends to stay awake and pray, but they fell asleep instead (Matthew 26:36–46). In Jesus's hour of need, when his closest friends let him down, Jesus resolutely returns to his Father and continues to pray.

When Paul was shipwrecked or imprisoned, he took comfort in God's presence and the prayers of believers, even though he was physically alone. Like Jesus, Paul turned to God amid many trials and afflictions. Paul was secure in God's love.

Scripture warns that you will face hardship, suffering, and affliction. But it also promises God's comfort (2 Corinthians 1:5). When you are lonely, turn first to God. Ask him to help you form friendships with believers at your church, even if they're different than the friends you're used to. Be open to whomever God provides, whether it's a trusted pastor or elder, an older church member, or another person in your youth group. Invite your church family to share your burden and encourage you.

When you suffer, draw strength from your identity in Christ as a comforted sufferer. Pray to God, who grieves with you and hears your prayers just as he heard Christ's in the garden. Read God's promises of comfort in his Word and wait eagerly for him to provide exactly what he knows you need.

The Father is with you, Christ understands you, and the Holy Spirit will comfort you in every affliction.

Ask: Has suffering tempted you to doubt who you are in Christ? Why?

Confess: Father, I confess my desire to avoid suffering. I foolishly attempt to change myself, my behavior, or my convictions in order to feel loved and accepted by others. Forgive me for the times I have avoided coming to you for comfort.

Discover: In Christ, I am comforted by God when I suffer.

Day 10

I AM FILLED WITH THE FULLNESS OF GOD'S GRACE

From his fullness we have all received, grace upon grace. (John 1:16)

In sixth-period study hall, Paige pulled out her phone to check her social media. She scrolled through photos of her friends: Kaitlin's gorgeous prom dress. Reagan's four college acceptance letters. Dillon's family vacation to Fiji. Paul and Jenny holding hands on their first official date.

Frustration overcame Paige as she turned off her phone and shoved it into her backpack. She wanted a swoon-worthy dress and stunning pictures like Kaitlin's. Her single college acceptance letter paled in comparison to Reagan's four. Her family never took fancy vacations like Dillon's. And would she ever have a boyfriend? The tiny, colorful photos stoked the emptiness and longing within Paige's heart.

Have you ever felt empty? Overlooked? Unfulfilled? Have you ever wondered if God is withholding his good gifts from you?

Think of what Scripture says about Jesus. Physically, he wasn't particularly handsome or impressive (Isaiah 53:2). As an adult, he had no home or possessions of his own (Luke 9:58). People mocked him, and his own friends betrayed him (Mark 14:43–50). He worked for no pay and didn't live luxuriously. And yet, the Father appointed Jesus as the head over all things, because in him, the fullness of God dwells and fills all in all (Ephesians 1:23).

God intends for his people to be fully satisfied in Christ, not in their physical appearance, relationships, or possessions.

John 1:14–16 explains that God sent his son Jesus, inviting us to see his glory and experience his grace. Grace means that God has given us what we did not deserve. We've glimpsed a blessing we had no right to see. When we were empty, God invited us to reap *his* goodness from *his* fullness. By grace, we received what we could not earn.

The Christian's sense of fulfillment isn't meant to be found in a highlight reel but in God, who directs every blessing.

Trendy clothes, exotic vacations, and popularity pale in comparison to the satisfaction we're meant to find in God's measureless grace. God isn't withholding his goodness when you lack a new smartphone or when you're left out of someone's trip. He knows the desires of your heart. But rather than giving you the latest and greatest gadget, he showers you with riches that are truly lasting and precious. Wisdom. Humility. Gentleness. A greater understanding of his character. Grace upon grace. God knows how to provide what you actually need, in order that you might come to value the riches of his mercy.

God gives out of his abundance, in order that you might be filled with his goodness and fully satisfied by him. In Christ, you are filled with the fullness of God's grace.

Ask: In what areas of your life do you doubt God's goodness? Where do you see evidence of Christ's love, even when you don't have what you want?

Confess: Lord, we confess that we are easily stirred to jealousy and envy. When we do not have what we think we should, we are quick to blame you or to question your faithfulness. When we long for the things of this world, help us to find full satisfaction in you and the provision we receive from your hand.

Discover: In Christ, I am confident that God's grace fills and satisfies my life with good.

WHAT IS MY PURPOSE?

Did you know that God has a grand purpose for you? This news might feel a little intimidating—like you're being called to come up with a way to support life on Mars. But surrendering yourself to God's purposes and plans isn't rocket science—it simply takes faith. As you follow Jesus, you will see that God's plans for you are good. Ephesians 2:10 says that we who are saved by grace, through faith, are God's "workmanship, created in Christ Jesus for good works, which God prepared beforehand, that we should walk in them."

In saving you by his grace, God sets you apart. He calls you to holiness and good works. Christ is both your perfect Savior and your perfect example. As you follow him, he will direct your steps and fill your life with meaning and purpose.

Rest in the assurance that God knows who you are in Christ and how to complete the good work he began in you.

This section highlights the unique ways that your identity in Christ provides you with purpose, all of which will help you become more like Jesus and accomplish his work.

.

Day 11

I AM A MEMBER OF GOD'S FAMILY

So then you are no longer strangers and aliens, but you are fellow citizens with the saints and members of the household of God, built on the foundation of the apostles and prophets, Christ Jesus himself being the cornerstone, in whom the whole structure, being joined together, grows into a holy temple in the Lord. In him you also are being built together into a dwelling place for God by the Spirit. (Ephesians 2:19–22)

When my friend entered her large liberal arts high school, her faith made her stand out like a sore thumb. Two years in, she still hadn't met another Christian there. And when she gathered with her small church on Sunday mornings, she stood out there too. She loved her church, but she was the only teenager in the congregation.

Differences have a way of dividing people into those who fit in and those who do not. Maybe you're a different ethnicity than most of the kids at your school. Or maybe you go to church with people whose parents make more money than yours do. Whatever it is that makes you different, it's easy to become fixated on your sense of being the odd one out.

Ephesians 2:19–22 teaches that God is building a new kind of temple. This new temple is made not out of physical stones but out of Christians. God joins us together in the local church—not by how we look or live but by our faith in Jesus. Inside the church, you're not alone; you belong to a body whose unity is founded upon your shared identity. You are all followers of Christ, called to gather with other believers for the purpose of growing and strengthening one another.

Whether or not you have an active youth group, connecting and contributing within your local church allows you to get to know the family of God, whatever age others may be.

While you and I may initially see all the differences that set us apart from one another, God places us together intentionally. We have so much in common when we all belong to Jesus and when we are all walking together toward holiness. Worshiping alongside people who are different from us challenges and encourages us to grow and mature in our faith. Inside the body of Christ, we all serve a purpose; we all have important work to do and roles to play. You need all of the people of God. And they all need you.

The Lord used my friend's challenging high school years to show her the importance of spiritual family. Her church welcomed and included her when her classmates rejected her. They didn't look down on her because of her age. She studied the Bible with adult women. She prayed aloud in church prayer meetings. She rocked babies in the nursery and sang on the praise team. As the church got to know her, they embraced her. She found a sense of belonging, even without a youth group or a gaga ball pit.

Teenagers are fellow members of God's household. You are important to the family. No matter what you look like, what you have to contribute, or who you know, you get the chance to find camaraderie and fellowship with believers of all ages inside the church. Bring your valuable skills, perspective, and gifts to God's people.

Your shared faith in Jesus is the glue that binds the family of God together into a *whole* structure and that builds us all into a holy temple of the Lord!

Ask: How could you invest in or contribute to your church? How might you spend time getting to know church members outside your youth group?

Confess: Lord, it is easy to feel self-conscious and to avoid spending time with the Christians in my local church. Forgive me for prioritizing my own comfort over loving others. Help me to become a vital, contributing member of my church community who finds joy in being a part of your family.

Discover: In Christ, I am a fellow citizen, saint, and member of the household of God.

I AM A GOSPEL STEWARD

This is how one should regard us, as servants of Christ and stewards of the mysteries of God. Moreover, it is required of stewards that they be found faithful. (1 Corinthians 4:1–2)

As a senior in high school and the captain of the football team, Kevin had been tasked with leading a student Bible study before school. Each week, the group gathered to eat donuts, read a Scripture passage, and pray together.

One morning, Kevin noticed Reid, the new kid from football, sitting in the back of the room. Reid was by far the smallest and slowest member of the team, and everyone knew it. In the locker room and on the field, Kevin and his teammates took every opportunity to torment him.

Now Kevin felt miserably uncomfortable sharing a message about the love and grace of Jesus in front of a guy he'd spent months harassing. He felt like such a hypocrite.

Have you ever been hesitant to share the hope you have in Jesus because of how your own life has failed to demonstrate Christ? Do you know how awkward it feels to realize you're a hypocrite?

We don't always live in ways that reflect or proclaim Jesus. When our actions contradict what we say we believe, we have a chance to return to the good news of our identity in Christ. The good news of the gospel is true, even when we have behaved badly. In fact, that's when we need the gospel the most.

First Corinthians 4:1–2 reminds believers that we have a purpose: we are servants of Christ. We are called to faithfully carry the message of the gospel. For many of us, this is a task that feels intimidating. But sharing the gospel of Jesus doesn't require a polished presentation or that we feel comfortable. You can faithfully serve Jesus and tell others about the gospel, no matter your skill or comfort level, right now.

Sharing the gospel is a good work that Jesus sets before all of his followers, not just adults or seminary graduates. This means that the only qualification you need to speak about Jesus is to believe in him. If you've received salvation by grace, through faith, you can share your faith without worrying that you're not good enough.

Your identity in Christ gives you the courage to face your own hypocrisy head-on! When you feel God's conviction, or when you worry that your behavior has harmed the witness of the gospel you proclaim, you can ask God for help to make things right. Apologizing to others for our sin and asking God to help us to change demonstrates that we truly depend on the gospel we proclaim.

Do you find yourself living in a way that seems to deny your faith in Jesus? Are you bound by a desire to fit in? Come to God and tell him about it. Ask for his help. He is already at work to make you more like Jesus, and he will change you from the inside out.

Ask: Do your actions match what you say you believe as a follower of Christ? What do you think would happen if you trusted God in those areas of disconnect?

Confess: Lord, I confess that I don't always behave in ways that demonstrate Christ's love or the good news of the gospel. Forgive me for the times in which I've hurt others or failed to serve you. Help me to be less self-centered so that I might faithfully serve you.

Discover: In Christ, I am set apart by God to be a faithful servant of the gospel.

I AM AN ACTIVE LABORER

The harvest is plentiful, but the laborers are few.
Therefore pray earnestly to the Lord of the harvest to
send out laborers into his harvest. (Luke 10:2)

I learned how to build a house as a ninth grader when our church's youth group partnered with Habitat for Humanity. I agreed to pack my duffel bag, ride in a van across the state, and sleep on the floor of another church's gym, all in order to build a home for a family in need.

It wasn't a particularly selfless endeavor. I didn't enjoy manual labor. I had no idea what I would be asked to do and no skills to speak of. I'd never built a wall. I didn't know what "taping and bedding" meant. I committed to this trip because I had a fear of missing out. If I'd realized how hot the summer sun would feel or how little downtime there'd be, I probably wouldn't have agreed to serve.

Miraculously, I showed up and worked. I learned how to use power tools, I helped frame the house, I put up drywall and painted. In one week, we turned an empty grass lot into a safe place for a family to sleep. And a marvelous thing happened inside my heart: I began to enjoy laboring for others.

In Luke 10:2, Jesus dispatched seventy-two of his followers to work among the people in the surrounding towns, declaring God's coming kingdom in order to gather true believers from the plentiful harvest. Today, we (the church) are God's skilled laborers, and we're continuing the same work. As we labor in various ways for the furtherance of the gospel, the Lord of the harvest gathers his people from every nation, building his spiritual house not of bricks and mortar but of redeemed saints who are bound together by the precious blood of Christ. How might God call you to labor too?

At this stage of life, teenagers are regularly encouraged to pursue their dream job in order to build their own life and identity.

But in Christ, you already have a God-given identity: you are a skilled worker, and you are called to enter the harvest on behalf of Christ. Every day, God takes your contributions and establishes your work to build his house.

You don't need a hammer to obediently labor alongside Jesus. Use your daily life, your choices, your conversations, your commitments, and your relationships to participate in the work of calling people to trust and follow Jesus. By his grace, this noble work of kingdom-building will last into eternity.

Ask: What might it look like for you to labor within the kingdom of God? What strengths or skills has God given you that can help you do the work of evangelism or discipleship?

Confess: Lord Jesus, I confess that I want to find my identity in my skills and work for my own glory. Forgive me for failing to use my gifts to labor for your kingdom. When I'm nervous to labor in your name, help me to be bold and courageous.

Discover: In Christ, I am an active laborer, and I have been sent into the field to gather the harvest.

I AM GROWING IN GODLINESS

*Him we proclaim, warning everyone and teaching
everyone with all wisdom, that we may present
everyone mature in Christ. (Colossians 1:28)*

My sons love to look back through old pictures of themselves. Documented for posterity are the days when Sillybandz lined their arms, or when they pulled white tube socks up so high that they looked like pants, or when they wore cowboy boots with shorts in the middle of winter. They even enjoy video clips of their toddler temper tantrums, mispronounced words, and painful first attempts to ride a bike.

We enjoy snapshots of the past because they show how much we've physically grown. If I looked back and noticed that my high school senior was still the size of a second grader, I would have a cause for concern. I would want to investigate why he wasn't growing and get to the root of the problem.

When it comes to spiritual maturity, do you enjoy looking back and observing how you've grown? Are you free from old sins? Do you enjoy spending time with other believers? When we are growing and maturing in our faith, we change over time.

But sometimes this growth occurs more slowly than we'd like. We may worry that we aren't growing at all. Maybe you struggle to read the Bible. Maybe there are sins you can't seem to shake. Maybe you fear that you'll never be as strong in your faith as other Christians you know.

Both at school and at home, greater maturity is often rewarded with greater privileges and blessings. But Christ Jesus has already secured every spiritual blessing you need to grow into maturity. That means you aren't on your own. God will help you grow. He will bring you to maturity according to his schedule, by his hand.

In Colossians 1:28, Paul urges Christians to proclaim Jesus, so that everyone would be warned and taught by the gospel and grow in faith and maturity. God most often grows his people through the proclamation and teaching of his Word. This is why worshipping with other believers and hearing God's Word together is so important.

God graciously helps us outgrow immaturity by making us more like Jesus. We grow in godliness as he makes us more and more holy, like he is. As you give your life to serving Jesus, God will grow you not by your willpower or your level of commitment but by his strength. The same God who called you when you were still his enemy will bring you to maturity in him.

When you look back a year or two from now, maybe you will realize you know God's Word better than you did before. Or maybe you will see how you have grown in a desire to spend time with other believers. Perhaps you will look back and see how God has helped you to exchange some of your anxiety and insecurity for peace and confidence in him. Entrust your growth to God and watch as the Holy Spirit helps you. If you've professed faith in Jesus, you're growing right now!

Don't just look back at how you've grown—look forward too. God will faithfully mature you all the way up to the day when Jesus presents you as fully blameless before his throne (Jude 1:24).

Ask: Have you taken pride in your Christian maturity or felt pressured to fake more maturity than you have? Why might that be a sign that you've placed your identity on the wrong foundation?

Confess: Lord, I confess that my desire to grow often arises from a desire to impress you or others. Help me to rest in my security in Christ so that I might persevere in becoming more mature.

Discover: In Christ, I am actively growing and maturing by the power of God.

Day 15

I AM WORD-FED

All Scripture is breathed out by God and profitable for teaching, for reproof, for correction, and for training in righteousness, that the man of God may be complete, equipped for every good work. (2 Timothy 3:16–17)

Something strange happened when my sons joined the high school football team: they suddenly began to care about eating healthy food.

Coach Pappy spent the beginning and end of every practice driving home the importance of nutrition. In order to get their bodies into peak performance condition, the players needed to eat and drink exactly as he directed. And so they did. Practically overnight, my sons began turning down sweets and sodas in favor of salad. They carried around gigantic water jugs and used their allowance money to buy vitamins and powdered hydration boosters. As they followed Pappy's directions, they grew stronger and more muscular.

These nutritional choices weren't alluring on their own. My sons needed to be convinced of their value before willingly surrendering their Cheetos. But when they believed that eating healthy food legitimately paid off, they agreed to make sacrifices.

When you trust someone, you listen to them. And when you believe them, you're willing to yield to their authority and direction.

Who do you allow to speak into your life? Are you listening to social media influencers? To friends at school? You're constantly invited to craft your own identity. You're asked to decide what you want to do in the coming days and years of your life. As you consider your options, where will you find wisdom?

In our verses for today, Paul urges young believers to yield themselves to the authority of God's Word because it has been breathed out by God for their benefit. God commands that we obey him, but he also demonstrates his love for us so that we will desire to listen to and trust in his Spirit.

God is the Author of Scripture. As we read and hear his Word, the Holy Spirit speaks, and he enables us to know and love God. As we learn to trust the truth of his Word, we want to obey his commands more and more because we believe he knows what is best for us. In the same way that my sons trusted Pappy's dietary advice (and even tried his weird kale smoothies), knowing God compels us to follow all of his Word—not just the parts we like.

Spend time reading God's Word. This is the primary way that you will learn who you are in Christ and how to live like Jesus.

If you don't understand what you're reading, or if you don't know where to look in order to answer your most important questions, seek the help of a trusted Bible teacher. Ask God to lead you by his Spirit into greater understanding. Be patient with yourself as you learn.

You were designed to hunger and thirst for Jesus because he alone is the bread of life (John 6:35). Come to the table. Approach his Word as the gloriously nutritious diet that it is, and you will be fully satisfied.

Ask: In what ways do your daily habits reveal whether you trust God as the Author of the Bible? Where can you grow in your understanding of Scripture?

Confess: Lord, I confess that it's easier to ignore your Word than to study and revere it. I am often tempted to neglect your commands or to turn away in shame. Forgive me and grant me a hunger for your truth.

Discover: In Christ, I am filled with knowledge and truth as God equips me through his Holy Word.

I AM SPIRIT-LED

For all who are led by the Spirit of God are sons of God.
For you did not receive the spirit of slavery to fall back into
fear, but you have received the Spirit of adoption as sons,
by whom we cry, "Abba! Father!" (Romans 8:14–16)

At this stage in your life, you're probably guided by adults. In everything from learning algebra to making major decisions, you're told to look to parents, teachers, coaches, and pastors who'll lead you in the way you should go.

But when you come to faith in Christ, God fills you with his Holy Spirit! He becomes your primary guide, and you must learn to listen for his instruction. He will lead you away from sin and into the good works God has prepared for you. This is often what Christians mean when they talk about the importance of being "led by the Spirit."

Of course, this isn't like being led by parents or teachers, with whom you can speak face-to-face. Asking God questions and listening for answers may feel awkward or intimidating. What if you mishear?

You might wish that following God's lead and listening to the Holy Spirit felt more like the game Simon Says. Wouldn't it be nice to have direct instructions on what to do or not do? *Don't go to the party. Do keep the secret for your friend. Don't play field hockey next season. Do spend your money on college.*

We want clear answers to personal questions so we can know for sure that we're pleasing God. We think that if God would speak to us directly, like he spoke to Moses in the burning bush (Exodus 3), then we'd feel assured of his loving, good plans for our life, after which we'd stop worrying.

When your identity is in Christ, though, it doesn't depend on whether *you* can perfectly discern and follow the Spirit's lead. You can walk by the Spirit as you rest in the gospel.

Romans 8:14–16 assures you that God blesses his children with the constant, indwelling presence of the Holy Spirit, so that you won't fall back into the fear that you're alone and helpless.

The truth is, when you belong to Jesus, you're loved and led, even as you follow the Spirit imperfectly. The Holy Spirit abides in you and directs you, whether or not you hear or understand him perfectly. You are secure in Christ. Don't panic when you can't discern God's still, small voice—just ask for his wisdom, without feeling embarrassed or doubting your salvation. Through his Word, the Spirit always directs the minds and hearts of his children.

You sense the Spirit's guidance by paying attention to how he stirs your conscience. As you read or reflect on God's Word, he assures you of his presence and his love. He instructs you to obey his commands, enables you to discern truth from lies, and grants you courage in times of trial. God leads you by his Spirit on purpose, so that you will learn to listen to and depend on him.

God the Father showed Jesus all that he was doing (John 5:20). Jesus heard him perfectly, and then he shared all that he's heard with you, so that you might now hear. John 8:47 reminds us that "whoever is of God hears the words of God." When you are in Christ, you are always Spirit-led. Will you listen?

Ask: What fears or burdens are you struggling with right now? Have you looked to the Holy Spirit for help? Where might you find his guidance?

Confess: God, I confess that I am unsure of how to listen for the Spirit's leading. Forgive me for failing to come to your Word, the Bible, to hear you speak. Teach me your words of life, that I might recognize your voice.

Discover: In Christ, I am filled with the Holy Spirit and led by the living God.

Day 17

I AM PURSUING PEACE

So flee youthful passions and pursue righteousness,
faith, love, and peace, along with those who call on
the Lord from a pure heart. (2 Timothy 2:22)

Jack and his best friend were thrilled when they qualified to compete in a state science competition. But after traveling ten hours from home and showing up with a carefully packed trifold presentation, Jack discovered that all the other projects looked far more impressive and elaborate than what he'd prepared.

Jack came up with a harebrained idea to tell the judges that their project had been destroyed right before the competition. If the trifold display standing before the judges was the best the boys could do in a pinch, Jack hoped that pulling on their heartstrings might win them a shot at advancing in the competition.

The truth is that even when you're filled with the Holy Spirit, who leads you in the right way, you don't always listen. Sometimes your outward actions don't match who you are in Christ.

Maybe you lash out in anger at your siblings. Or maybe you disregard the boundaries your parents have put in place for dating. Or maybe your social media or video gaming habits have grown increasingly unhealthy, but you're happy to live in denial. In today's verse, Paul calls Christians to flee—to quickly run away in the opposite direction—from any impulsive, "youthful passion" that distracts us from honoring and obeying God or that tempts us to break God's commands.

Instead, we sometimes hesitate to do what we know is right. And when we experience guilt or shame as a result, it's often because we're ignoring the Holy Spirit's voice of conviction.

Willfully and repeatedly participating in sin prevents us from resting in our identity in Christ. Because Jesus freed us from the

49

power of sin, we can confidently ask him for help in order to flee those pesky temptations and live righteously, as we really are.

Jack didn't need to win a science competition to feel good about himself. As a follower of Jesus, he has the fullness of God's love, even with an unimpressive trifold project. In the moment of his temptation, a confident understanding of his identity in Christ could have helped him to recognize the foolishness of cheating, to turn away from evil, and to pursue righteousness—knowing that pleasing the Lord and finding his acceptance in Christ would be more valuable than winning.

Because of who you are in Jesus, you don't have to make a name for yourself by walking in sinful paths. Instead, you are freed to do what is right and faithful.

The Holy Spirit empowers you to live according to your new identity in Christ, pursuing righteousness, faith, love, and peace alongside those who call on the Lord from a pure heart.

Ask: In what areas of your life is the Spirit urging you to turn away from sin? How might you flee from sin and run toward Jesus today?

Confess: Lord, I confess that I want to be known for my accomplishments and that sometimes I'm willing to sin in order to get what I want. Forgive me for valuing my reputation over obedience to your commands.

Discover: In Christ, I am empowered by God to flee sin and to pursue righteousness.

Day 18

I AM PERSEVERING UNDER PERSECUTION

All who desire to live a godly life in Christ Jesus will be persecuted, while evil people and impostors will go on from bad to worse.... But as for you, continue in what you have learned and have firmly believed, knowing from whom you learned it and how from childhood you have been acquainted with the sacred writings, which are able to make you wise for salvation through faith in Christ Jesus. (2 Timothy 3:12–15)

Dara had always spoken openly about her faith at school. And even though her classmates weren't Christians, they'd never seemed to mind when she expressed her beliefs. So, when she approached the lunch table and noticed that her friends hadn't left an open seat for her, she still expected them to scoot over and make some room.

But they didn't budge. Instead, one of the girls said, "We've decided that we don't want to be friends with religious people anymore. You're too closed-minded. We don't need your negativity." And with that, they went back to eating their sandwiches.

In the weeks that followed, the girls' behavior became increasingly antagonistic. They publicly shunned Dara and began to spread rumors about her. In class, they took every opportunity to mock her beliefs. Now Dara wonders if she should have kept quiet about her faith.

Have you ever been rejected, or even hated, because you follow Jesus? If so, you're not alone—he was persecuted too.

Your identity in Christ ensures that a glorious salvation awaits you in heaven, but it also means walking the path of rejection and suffering right now. We live in a world marked by sin and brokenness. You are fully loved and accepted by God, but don't be surprised when people who do not know Christ hate or reject you. Persecution is a fact of life for those whose identity is in Jesus.

Second Timothy 3:12–15 warns that if you desire to live a godly life, you should expect to encounter suffering, trials, and evildoers! But as you do, stand firm in your faith. Persecution never feels easy, but the Spirit will use it to draw you closer to Christ.

You don't need to prove how strong you are in the face of an attack. You aren't an emotionless robot. And Jesus isn't disappointed when you feel hurt and rejected by your friends. He understands how betrayal feels, and he desires to draw you in and comfort you. As the pain of persecution purifies and strengthens your faith, recall the good news that you are deeply loved by Christ.

Ask: Have you ever been shunned, rejected, or dismissed because of your faith? If so, how did you react?

Confess: Lord, I confess that I am too easily offended and hurt. I want following you to feel easy and painless. Forgive me, Lord, when I blame you for my distress instead of looking to you for comfort.

Discover: In Christ, I am able to persevere by God's strength when I suffer persecution.

I AM HELPED AND HUMBLED

Christ Jesus . . . though he was in the form of God, did not count equality with God a thing to be grasped, but emptied himself. . . . And being found in human form, he humbled himself by becoming obedient to the point of death, even death on a cross. (Philippians 2:5–8)

As our family of seven gathered around the breakfast table for a meeting, half of us arrived grumpy and tired. Some hadn't had their coffee. A brother fight broke out. Someone wouldn't put away their phone. Finally, having had enough of my teenagers' constant bickering, I lashed out at everyone in the mommest-of-mom voices I could summon: *"Guys. This is ridiculous. Knock it off. Why can't you treat one another kindly? Do you hear yourself? Are you speaking with the love and gentleness of Jesus?!"*

Conviction immediately swept over me. Was I treating my teenagers kindly? Was I speaking with the love and gentleness of Jesus? Oooof. No, I was not. The last thing I wanted to do was apologize, but I had to. I needed to repent of my poor attitude and my self-righteous posture. Today, apologizing to my family and asking their forgiveness was the good work God had set before me. But doing so required me to humble myself.

Have you ever made excuses for your sinful behavior instead of owning up to it and apologizing? Humility is hard work. But Jesus helps us put on this new identity.

When Jesus's disciples asked him, "Who is the greatest in the kingdom of heaven?" (Matthew 18:1), he certainly could have been frustrated by their self-centered immaturity. But Jesus took their question seriously and told them, "Whoever humbles himself . . . is the greatest in the kingdom of heaven" (verse 4).

Jesus is the perfect example of humility. Rather than striving to be the greatest, he emptied himself to take on human flesh

(Philippians 2:1–11). And after living a difficult life of service and sacrifice, he willingly died for his people so that their sins would be forgiven.

When you notice sin or selfishness in your life (like I did that morning with my family), remember Jesus, who gave himself for you on the cross. He will help you to grow and to serve others.

When you are confident of your identity in Christ, you don't have to be afraid of admitting when you're wrong. Remember, you aren't defined by being right—you're defined by the fact that you belong to Jesus. You can apologize for gossiping about a friend or for dishonoring your parents, knowing that in Christ you're already forgiven.

As you grow in humility, remember that Jesus didn't harp on his equality with God when he became flesh. Instead, he humbled himself and entered the world as a baby. He didn't fear dependence but fully relied on his Father. He spent his time serving others, not being served. Jesus modeled humility, and, when we trust in him, we receive the record of his humble service.

As saved sinners, we have every reason to live humbly with God and with others, because we depend on God's grace and Christ's forgiveness.

Ask: Where in your life do you tend to feel proud or boastful? How might God be working to humble you?

Confess: Lord, we confess our temptation to prove our own righteousness to you and to others. We want to earn our place in your kingdom instead of rejoicing that we've been granted it by grace. Forgive us for our pride. Help us to gratefully receive the gift of your gospel and to walk humbly in your grace.

Discover: In Christ, I am humbled by the grace of God given to me through the good news of the gospel.

I AM RELIANT ON GOD'S GRACE

For by grace you have been saved through faith. And this is not your own doing; it is the gift of God, not a result of works, so that no one may boast. (Ephesians 2:8–9)

I entered high school keenly aware of all that I was not. I wasn't popular or good at math, and I didn't have an athletic bone in my body. When teachers noticed that I could act and sing, I hopped on stage and settled into the fine-arts family for the next four years.

Performing earned me accolades and approval. But it also made me feel constantly insecure. While I felt seen and valued for my contributions on the stage, I was also terrified of forgetting lines, singing off pitch, or giving a poor performance. I labored under the fear that at any moment I could fail and lose the acceptance I found from the stage.

That day eventually arrived. Erin showed up during my senior year, and her talent far exceeded my own. She was an incredibly talented actress, singer, and dancer. I couldn't compete with her. So, I became an insecure mess who constantly worried that losing leading roles meant losing the love of my teachers and my friends. When I wasn't the best, I doubted my value and worth. Can you relate?

If you suddenly lost the ability to perform, play, compete, or do whatever earns you love and acceptance, would you still feel confident in who you are? We often seek approval and direction from other people. When we look to others in this way—turning to those whose opinions and preferences are ever-changing—we will always feel unstable. In order to confidently rest in who we are in Christ, we must find our validation and worth in him alone.

Ephesians 2:8–9 assures us that Christians are saved by grace alone, through faith alone. You aren't rescued and redeemed by God because you're talented or impressive. God welcomes you into his family without taking *your performance* into consideration. You have been planted firmly in the kingdom of God because of God's gift of grace through his Son. Because you did nothing to earn your place, you can do nothing to lose it.

This means that you can find confidence in Jesus, even when you aren't the best or the most talented. When you notice the gifts and skills of others, steady your heart with the unshifting goodness of Jesus. Thank him that your sense of identity and worth does not depend on you.

Security in Christ frees you from boasting in your own abilities. Just as you rejoice that your salvation is a free gift, rejoice that all your skills and talents are gifts of grace too. Acknowledge what you're good at without boasting. Then, get to work using your skills for God's glory. When you see your abilities as gifts of grace rather than identity markers, you can labor in joyful service.

God's free gifts of grace grant you all sufficiency, in all things, at all times. Rely on the grace of Jesus. Thank God that you've found your fit in Christ forevermore.

Ask: Is there a skill or a talent that you rely on in order to find acceptance from God or from others? What do you think might change if you relied on God's grace instead?

Confess: Lord, I confess that I work hard to prove myself because I haven't learned to rest in your grace. Forgive me for acting as if Christ's sacrifice isn't enough and for trying to earn your love. Help me to rejoice in your free gift of grace.

Discover: In Christ, I am reliant on God's grace.

HOW DOES WHO I AM IMPACT HOW I LIVE?

One afternoon, I drove to a stranger's house to pick up a piece of furniture I bought online. From the edge of the driveway, a smiling man in a wheelchair greeted me and pointed to the item I'd come to retrieve. Then he sat watching me as I clumsily loaded it into my car.

As I slammed the trunk closed, the man literally hopped up from his wheelchair, sprinted across the driveway, and waved goodbye. As I stared, he glanced at the wheelchair, then back at me, and said, "Oh, that? I got it at a yard sale yesterday. I don't actually need it."

I'd been duped. But why? Why would someone who could run pretend he could not even stand? Who you are ought to impact how you live.

When you come to faith in Christ, you are healed and made whole, freed from the power of sin, and raised to walk in the newness of life. Why pretend sin or insecurity still defines you? You have God's Spirit within you to help you walk by faith and obey God's commands. The Holy Spirit will fill your heart with his fruit—love, joy, peace, patience, kindness, goodness, faithfulness, gentleness, and self-control—by his grace (Galatians 5:22–23).

In the remaining readings, we will consider how your new identity in Christ impacts how you live each and every day. When you are rooted in God's love through the work of Christ, the Holy Spirit makes your life fruitful. He makes you more like Jesus.

I AM FILLED TO ABOUND

It is my prayer that your love may abound more and more, with knowledge and all discernment, so that you may approve what is excellent, and so be pure and blameless for the day of Christ, filled with the fruit of righteousness that comes through Jesus Christ, to the glory and praise of God. (Philippians 1:9–11)

At my church, junk food flows freely. Donuts on the welcome counter. Sodas and desserts at Wednesday night youth events. Potluck dinners. Our teenagers love to sing the praises of those who provide the goodies.

One of my sugar-addicted sons showed up to church on Sunday morning and was delighted to find gigantic candy-filled tubs all over the building. He wanted nothing more than to fill his pockets.

Much to his disappointment, however, these tubs were donation bins for an upcoming community outreach event meant to bless the neighborhood kids. Church members who didn't have much income to spare had sacrificially scraped together extra grocery money to serve the church's greater mission. The containers overflowed with candy because our members' hearts overflowed with love for their neighbors. Now the church would have countless opportunities to meet them and to share the good news of the gospel.

Before I could slip into a lecture about selfless giving, my son asked if I would take him to the store after church so that he could use some of his lawn-mowing money to buy a bag of candy to contribute. I was delighted to see him respond to the Holy Spirit's prompting. In Christ, we become givers instead of takers.

In Philippians 1:9–11, Paul exhorts followers of Jesus to abound in love so that we may advance the gospel (v. 12). When we receive the good news of Jesus, the Holy Spirit fills our lives with his fruit, which abundantly increases *for the good of others* and for the glory of God.

Paul prayed often that followers of Jesus would "abound" in the fruit of the Spirit in order to build up the kingdom of God. In Colossians 1:3–6, he prayed and gave thanks for the glorious result: the gospel was "bearing fruit and increasing" (verse 6). Your new identity as a Christian transforms how you see the needs of others and contribute to the world around you. You are filled to abound in increasing measure so that you can help build up God's kingdom and strengthen God's people!

Is the fruit of the Spirit evident in your life? Are you eager to abound in this fruit for the sake of others?

Jesus tells us that the world will know us by our love (John 13:35). He compels us to overflow with love—in the form of coffee, candy, time, or attention—because acts of love make genuine faith evident for all to see.

Jesus provided for you out of the riches of his abundance. Now that you are in Christ, the Holy Spirit will fill you with his fruit, that you might selflessly love others and contribute to their needs out of your newfound abundance.

> **Ask:** Can you think of a time when you saw the fruit of the Spirit on display in another Christian's life? How did that fruit bless you? What spiritual fruit have you seen in your life since you came to faith?
>
> **Confess:** Lord, I confess that it's easier to take than it is to give. Forgive me for the ways in which I use your gifts to serve myself rather than my neighbor. Help me understand how I can share the gospel with others, that they might come to know the love of Christ.
>
> **Discover:** In Christ, I am filled with the fruit of the Spirit for the good of others.

I AM LOVED AND LOVING

Love is patient and kind; love does not envy or boast; it is not arrogant or rude. It does not insist on its own way; it is not irritable or resentful; it does not rejoice at wrongdoing, but rejoices with the truth. Love bears all things, believes all things, hopes all things, endures all things. (1 Corinthians 13:4–7)

As a teenager who wanted to be loved, I struggled to love others. I measured love by how many friends I had, how many boys wanted to date me, and how included I felt. Inevitably, girl drama and failed relationships convinced me that I was unlovable.

Maybe you understand love better than I did. But you live in a brutal cancel culture that takes a massive toll on your heart. It's dehumanizing to be dropped or shamed by others. When you extend love to a friend, only to be rejected, ghosted, blocked, or forgotten, it's easy to believe that love isn't worth the hassle.

If the decision to love others were only up to us, we might steer clear just to avoid being hurt.

Christians, however, are called to extend a love that's unlike the transitory, conditional love we find in the world. God's love sought us out when we were totally unlovable. Christ's love sacrificed for the good of sinners. Now, it continues to carry us even through our sin and immaturity.

Jesus told a story about a father and two sons to illustrate God the Father's great love for us (Luke 15:11–32). The older son dutifully serves his father, while the younger son runs away with his inheritance and spends it recklessly. Out of cash and desperate, the younger son returns home, hoping his father will let him work as a slave. But when his father sees him, he runs to him, forgives him, and throws an expensive celebration to welcome him home as his beloved son. Jesus wanted us to know that God's love for us is not dependent on what we do. He went to the cross and died for us because his love is perfectly forgiving and selfless.

If you've ever tried to love others like this, you've noticed that it's impossible to do on your own. We require supernatural help from God. Love is a fruit of the Spirit, which means God increasingly produces it in our lives as we trust in him.

When our source of identity remains firmly rooted in Christ, we can love others without the fear of rejection because we have the abiding love of the Father. Christ's love remains, even if all our friends abandon us.

The Holy Spirit will help you love your friend who gossips or who isn't a good listener. He will deepen your love for people you don't understand or relate to. When loving others feels painful and impossible, remember that the Spirit is at work within you, cultivating the fruit of love in your life so that you will show others the selfless love of Christ.

> **Ask:** Have you ever struggled to feel loved by God because a person failed to love you? Who have you struggled to love?
>
> **Confess:** Father, I confess that I have not loved others as myself. Teach me to love like Jesus!
>
> **Discover:** In Christ, I know the love of Jesus, and I'm filled with the fruit of the Spirit in order to share God's love with others.

I AM FILLED WITH JOY

May the God of hope fill you with all joy and peace
in believing, so that by the power of the Holy Spirit
you may abound in hope. (Romans 15:13)

Joy isn't what I feel when my alarm clock goes off in the morning. Sometimes I feel dread. Annoyance. Frustration. I want to silence the shrill beeping, roll over, and go back to sleep. But when I look to Jesus and think of all he has done for me, I find that God gives me his joy even in the midst of hard circumstances.

Every day, you face your own set of expectations and opportunities that can fill you with a sense of joy or drain you of it. Contentment is easy when you make the team, when you find a homecoming date, or when you earn a scholarship. But it's fleeting when bad grades render you unable to compete on the team, or when your date breaks up with you, or when your family can't afford to send you to college. When joy depends on your circumstances or your emotions, it will always feel unstable.

God helps his people by giving us a joy that will last for the long haul. But this doesn't mean that we'll always feel like Sam or Suzy Sunshine. Because we are beloved disciples of Christ Jesus, we are meant to draw our sense of pleasure and delight from being known and loved by God the Father. This good news *never changes*!

Christ—who remains the same yesterday, today, and tomorrow (Hebrews 13:8)—is your very present source of forgiveness, salvation, deliverance, and reward. Therefore, you always have a reason to hope in him. This good news is meant to fill your heart with lasting joy.

Joy is a result of the Holy Spirit's work in you. It isn't something you drum up through your own efforts—rather, it takes time to grow. It is planted like a seed, and by the Spirit's power, it will flourish over the course of your life. Joy isn't just a happy feeling—it's an enduring expression of gratitude for what Christ has done in your life.

Christian joy also bears an attractive witness to others. Think of how amazed and perplexed unbelievers may be when joy blossoms within hardship. When home life is difficult. When your grades are tanking. When your boss hates you. Throughout all these trials, joy can be yours, even as pain abounds—for your source of satisfaction is your unchanging Savior, not your unstable circumstances.

You can't produce lasting joy by your own strength, but you can ask God for it. On days when you feel frustrated and unhappy, even guilty and ashamed, ask him to help you to draw joy from your identity as a follower of Jesus. Read through a psalm. Sing a song of praise in your car. Make a gratitude bullet list in your journal. Be honest with God about your emotions and pray that he would fill you "with all joy and peace," which flow from your salvation in Jesus, not your circumstances.

Ask: When do you feel joyless? What are a few truths about Jesus that could fill you with joy amid suffering?

Confess: Lord, I confess that I wrongly look to my circumstances for happiness instead of looking to you for lasting joy. Forgive me for being so easily satisfied with that which does not last.

Discover: In Christ, I am filled with the fruit of the Spirit so that I might know and share the lasting joy that comes from my salvation.

I AM STILL AND PEACEFUL

Peace I leave with you; my peace I give to you. Not as the world gives do I give to you. Let not your hearts be troubled, neither let them be afraid. (John 14:27)

Jamar never imagined that his senior year of high school could be so stressful. Every morning, he went to school early for weight lifting and stayed late for practices or tutoring. Between homework and working to save money for college, he rarely felt the freedom to relax. Each night, his stomach felt tense as his mind drifted from one anxiety to the next.

At youth group one day, Jamar's leader read Jesus's words to his disciples: "Peace I leave with you; my peace I give to you." Peace? Jamar wasn't sure when he'd last felt peaceful. Maybe third grade?

How was he supposed to experience the peace he'd been given through Christ? He considered how much he worried about pleasing his coach. And how much he obsessed over his grades. And how little money he'd saved for college.

Jamar often felt that it was up to him to off-load his anxieties. This sense of responsibility only added additional worry. Should he quit the team? Or get a tutor? Or pick up some extra shifts at work? The more he tried to come up with solutions, the more anxious he felt.

Jamar wanted to cast all his cares on the Lord, but even when he prayed and told God how he felt, he still didn't *feel* peaceful.

Can you relate? Maybe you desire peace, but you regularly feel worried. Do you assume that finding peace depends on you? Can a Christian feel anxious or worried and still rest in the peace that Jesus provides?

As a follower of Jesus, your identity isn't found in how you feel moment to moment. Christ isn't angry with you when you fail to remain perfectly calm in all circumstances. In fact, he is filled with compassion, and he desires to help you. As you come to him, he will give you his peace, by his strength. The fruit of peace is a work of the Holy Spirit.

One time, Jesus was in a boat with his disciples, and a storm sprung up. The disciples were certain they would all die. Jesus woke up, commanded the storm to be still, and the seas obeyed. Even then, the men still felt afraid (Mark 4:35–41).

Before his death, Jesus warned his disciples that he was going away (for example, Matthew 16:21–23). He didn't want their hearts to be weighed down by anxiety after his death. Jesus spoke to his disciples before his crucifixion, in order to assure them that his peace could be theirs, even when he wasn't physically present with them. Because he would send the Holy Spirit as their helper, their hearts needn't be troubled (John 14:15–17).

When you are anxious or afraid, ask Jesus to help you. Plead for the Spirit to grant you the fruit of peace. Trust Jesus to care for you and surrender your burdens to him. Seek the peace of God by reading the Psalms and by finding assurance in God's provision. Memorize Scripture passages that reassure you of God's care for you.

Because of who you are in Jesus, you have the compassion of Jesus and the help of the Holy Spirit. He will produce the fruit of peace.

Ask: Are you tempted to produce a more peaceful life on your own? Do you pray for God's peace?

Confess: Lord, I confess that I often try to achieve peace on my own. Forgive me for finding my identity in how well I handle my anxieties. Help me to receive the peace you provide.

Discover: In Christ, I am filled with the fruit of the Spirit so that I can experience God's peace and pray for peace for others.

I AM PATIENT IN SUFFERING

Behold, we consider those blessed who remained steadfast. You have heard of the steadfastness of Job, and you have seen the purpose of the Lord, how the Lord is compassionate and merciful. (James 5:11)

Jane came to faith in Jesus three months before her mother lost her job. Now her mom didn't have the income to pay for things Jane had always taken for granted. Groceries were sparse. She needed new running shoes for school. She didn't get an allowance anymore, and she couldn't go out to eat with her friends.

As a new believer, Jane knew that she should love and honor her mother even when she felt frustrated. She prayed regularly for God to help her mom find a job. She knew God would care for their family; they had never run out of food, and their bills had somehow always been paid. But Jane couldn't shake her impatience with God. She wanted this trial to be over, now!

We like to believe that we will follow Jesus through trials of all kinds. But when reality hits, and life feels hard, we are often shocked by how much we struggle to endure.

Patience isn't a virtue at which anyone naturally excels. We don't like to be told that we must slow down and wait on the Father. We hate sitting still in uncertainty; we want immediate answers and resolution. We want control. What circumstances do you hope will pass quickly? Is there a burden you are ready to finish carrying? Where are you lacking patience?

James 5 asks believers to consider the "steadfastness," or *patience*, of Job. In the midst of all the tragedy and loss Job experienced, his suffering yielded the fruit of patience. This doesn't mean he just suffered quietly—he was honest with God about his pain. The Lord answered him and came to his aid. He will help you too.

When you feel impatient amid your own circumstances, talk to God. Don't be shy: ask him to provide for your needs, but include patience as one of those needs. Practice patience by resisting the urge to take control or to immediately solve all your problems. Waiting on the Lord—and simply praying—is often the best way to learn patience in situations where you feel confused and helpless. Ask the Lord for help as you walk by the Spirit, with the steadfast endurance of Job.

You need the Spirit's intervention to yield yourself to God. But because you've been filled with the fruit of the Spirit, you are enabled to grow in Christlike patience, even when you feel impatient. God, who is patient with sinners, will surely produce patience within you!

Ask: What trial are you currently facing that requires patience? Have you tried praying for God's grace as you wait? Why or why not?

Confess: Lord, I confess that I want help, answers, and control more than I want to grow in the fruit of the Spirit. Forgive me for the times when I doubt your love. Produce the fruit of patience in my heart as I look to you.

Discover: In Christ, I am filled with the fruit of the Spirit in order to patiently endure trials and suffering.

I AM KIND IN WORDS AND DEEDS

Or do you presume on the riches of his kindness and forbearance and patience, not knowing that God's kindness is meant to lead you to repentance? (Romans 2:4)

Have you ever bitten into a piece of fruit that you expected to taste sweet and delicious but that actually tasted bitter and disgusting? Or have you ever grabbed the wrong drink and been caught off guard by a surprising flavor? It's startling.

In a gimmick that I assume was designed to entertain, a popular candy company released a bag of jelly beans containing a variety of disgusting flavors like Dirty Dishwater, Stink Bug, Dead Fish, Spoiled Milk, Barf, Toothpaste, Liver and Onions, Stinky Socks, and Old Bandage. People began to mix normal beans with the nasty beans and then to trick one another into eating flavors that would make them want to vomit. No thanks, I'll pass.

Who enjoys being promised something sweet and then receiving something putrid? No one. But this is often how Christians treat others. We claim to follow Christ and love him, but our words can be biting and bitter.

Consider how our culture encourages us to use sarcasm. Our favorite TV characters often communicate with biting jabs, insults, and one-liners. It's an entire language in which we become fluent by the time we hit puberty. But is this how you want other people to talk to you? It's hard to admit your sin or confess a spiritual need to those whose words are sharp or cruel. God's love is patient and kind; it is not rude (1 Corinthians 13:4–7).

Scripture calls us to be kind. Have you ever noticed how difficult it is to do that? We can feel like we're failing left and right because in our own strength, we're not very kind. This is why we need Jesus.

In Romans 2:4, Christians are exhorted not to take God's kindness for granted but to remember how his kindness led us to repentance. In light of God's kindness and his instruction to become like Jesus, we must put on kindness too. We can't call people to the kindness of God and then flip the script. We need the Spirit's help to put on kindness so that we can extend God's kindness to others, whether or not we feel like they deserve it. This is the way of Jesus.

When the fruit of kindness grows abundantly in our lives, our words and actions won't ring hollow. But when we overflow with bitterness, the world is sure to doubt the sincerity of our love and the power of our gospel to transform hearts. When the Holy Spirit sanctifies us by the truth of his Word, he empowers us to accurately convey who we are in Christ and to demonstrate the sweet reality that the Lord is kind in all his works (Psalm 145:17).

The Holy Spirit will produce the fruit of kindness within you. It may not always look like what you'd expect. God tells the truth, even when it's unpopular, because that is kind. But he speaks truth with grace. Now that you are in Christ, the Spirit empowers you to be kind in your words, even when others aren't.

As the Holy Spirit produces kindness within your heart, surrender to him all your words, actions, and attitudes. Ask the Lord to search your heart, to remove bitterness, and to fill you with goodness, so that you can be kind to others and glorify him.

Ask: How can the words of a believer show you the kindness of God? Can you think of some examples from your own life?

Confess: Lord, I confess that I am often unkind in my thoughts, words, and actions. Forgive me for the times when I have valued humor over kindness toward others.

Discover: In Christ, I am filled with the fruit of the Spirit so that the kindness of God would be seen by all.

I AM GOOD TO OTHERS

*And God is able to make all grace abound to you, so
that having all sufficiency in all things at all times, you
may abound in every good work. (2 Corinthians 9:8)*

Have you ever tried to do something good in order to impress
others? Maybe you lent money to a classmate to gain their friendship. Maybe you never miss an assignment so that your teacher
will give you a good grade. We often imagine that to be good, we
must *do* good.

In Scripture, to be good is to be morally right in the eyes of
God and, therefore, rightfully desirable. Your identity as a Christian
is based on God's grace, not your own moral standing. When you
trusted in Jesus, you received his goodness without earning it by
your works. As the Spirit fills you with God's goodness, your heart
ought to overflow, spreading his goodness to others.

What makes you agree to help someone? What leads you to
spend your money to bless a friend? What convinces you to share
the gospel with a classmate despite your anxiety? *Goodness.*

Paul encourages the Christians in Corinth to trust that God
is able to produce the fruit of the Spirit by his grace, giving them
all they need so that they might flourish in doing good to others.
Jesus didn't give you his goodness so that you can prove yourself
to God or impress other people. He gave you his goodness as part
of your unearned salvation.

Goodness—just like the other fruit of the Spirit—is not something you can conjure up. You can't be good apart from Christ, and
you can't consistently do the right thing apart from the Spirit's
enabling power. As you receive goodness from God, your desires
change. You thirst for what is good, and once you receive it, you
want to share it with the world around you. God produces goodness in us so that we can point others to him, not to ourselves.

Even before the foundation of the world, God prepared good works for you to walk in (Ephesians 2:10), including loving others as yourself (Mark 12:31), providing for the needs of others, especially other Christians (Galatians 6:10), proclaiming the gospel to unbelievers (Matthew 28:18–20), and serving within your local church (1 Peter 4:9–11). Imagine how your perspective might shift if, instead of trying to "be good" by your own strength, you rested in your identity in Christ and asked God how he's uniquely positioned you to do good to your friends, your family, and your neighbors—all in the name of Jesus and by the Spirit's enabling power.

As you overflow with the fruit of the Spirit, you join in the good work of spreading God's goodness to everyone within your sphere of influence.

Ask: Who have you been building up recently, and how? Your good service is a sign of the Holy Spirit's work within you! For what good works has God uniquely equipped you? Who has he placed in your life for you to help?

Confess: Father, forgive me for trying to be good in order to impress you or to earn your love. I confess that I often seek the good of others for my own selfish purposes. Please forgive me, and please fill me with the fruit of the Spirit for the sake of others.

Discover: In Christ, I am filled with the fruit of the Spirit so that God's goodness would overflow from my life and bless others through the good works God has called me to do.

I AM GENTLE LIKE JESUS

Brothers and sisters, if anyone is caught in any transgression, you who are spiritual should restore him in a spirit of gentleness. (Galatians 6:1)

One Wednesday night during the summer, Brandon and Libby's youth group gathered at a church member's pool. From the back corner, a group of rowdy middle schoolers sent a wet volleyball hurtling across the pool and right into Libby's forehead. Over the next ten minutes, the boys hit three more people, spiking a final blow into Brandon's jaw. Instead of apologizing, they laughed and carried on.

Frustrated, Brandon approached the group and addressed them calmly: "Hey man, I'm not sure if you meant to do that, but it really hurt. And maybe you didn't notice, but you've hit several people. Could you knock it off?" But the boys laughed and ignored him. As much as Brandon wanted revenge, he resisted the urge to punch the fruit fly–sized kid or to push him into the pool.

In Galatians 6, Paul urges Christians to correct others with gentleness, not punches. But even as followers of Jesus, we can struggle to be gentle both when our anger is righteous and when it's not. Remember, gentleness is a fruit not of the flesh but of the Spirit (Galatians 5:22–23).

Once when Jesus was teaching his followers, he described himself as "gentle and lowly in heart" (Matthew 11:29). Think for a moment about how you responded the last time someone wronged you. Maybe you're thinking, "I can't be gentle like Jesus . . . it's not in my nature!" Friend, it's not natural for any of us.

Gentleness wasn't in the apostle Paul's DNA either. Actually, Paul was the opposite of gentle before Christ saved him—he persecuted and murdered Christians (Acts 8:1–3). The Spirit radically transformed Paul's heart and filled him with a supernatural ability to be gentle with the weak, just as Jesus had been gentle with him (Acts 9:1–9).

When God makes you new in Christ, he intends for his love to shape every aspect of your life. His love is patient, kind, and *gentle*. If you have grown up in a home where the gentleness of Jesus isn't regularly on display, look within your local church. You might begin by observing gentleness in your pastor or your elders, or you might ask a wise older member to mentor you and to teach you strategies for dealing with anger or frustration.

The Spirit will help you, no matter how foreign the concept of gentleness may feel, because gentleness is one of his fruits. God will enable you to be gentle like Jesus, even when it feels unnatural. And as he does, you will bless others with the gentleness of Christ.

We pursue gentleness not in order to avoid conflict or punishment but in order to represent Christ. Ask God to fill you with the fruit of the Spirit, including gentleness, so that you might generously show others the mercy of Jesus.

Ask: In what situations do you currently struggle to be gentle? Why do you think those situations are especially difficult?

Confess: Father, I confess that my thoughts, words, and actions often lack gentleness. Forgive me for displaying unrighteous anger instead of Christlike love. By your Spirit, show me how to speak and behave more gently before others.

Discover: In Christ, I am filled with the fruit of the Spirit so that I would show forth the gentleness of Jesus.

Day 29

I AM SELF-CONTROLLED THROUGH THE SPIRIT

For this reason I remind you to fan into flame the gift of God . . . for God gave us a spirit not of fear but of power and love and self-control. (2 Timothy 1:6–7)

Whitney confessed to her discipleship group that recently her relationship with God felt "off." She didn't feel as joyful as she did after coming home from summer camp. She didn't enjoy attending church. She had little interest in reading her Bible or spending time in prayer. She'd only attended today's group because her mom insisted.

The small group leader asked her how she'd spent time getting to know the Lord over the past month. She asked what Whitney had been doing to guard her mind in Christ. Whitney was ashamed to admit that she hadn't done much of anything—the only thing she'd guarded was her nightly Netflix binges.

At first, she'd told herself that she didn't have time to read the Bible because she was busy with school. But if she were honest, she wasn't too busy to spend time messaging friends or scrolling through endless reels. She knew something needed to change, and she felt guilty for binging on media, but not God's Word. But if she admitted this to her small group, they'd think less of her.

Have you ever considered that when you feel apathetic toward the Lord, it could be because you're indulging in too much TV, social media, or other entertainment? More than lacking motivation or desire, you may lack self-control.

In today's verse, Paul encourages believers to remember that God has given us a spirit of power, love, and self-control—so we need not fear. We can ask for his help when we are weak.

God is with you even when you struggle with addiction or other damaging behavior. You'll never be too far off for the Holy Spirit

75

to intervene and lead you back to obedience. He will empower you to do what is right. And because of Christ's sacrifice, you need not feel ashamed. When you confess your sins to God, the Holy Spirit will help you to flee sin and walk in his ways.

When Paul wrote to Timothy, he urged him to do *what he could* to fan his faith into flame. He didn't guilt him into working harder or being more self-controlled by his own strength, because he understood that denying the flesh and living in wisdom are works of the Spirit.

Turning away from sin or overindulgence requires self-discipline and sacrifice. It's hard work, but God is with you and is working in you. When you seek to obey him with your thoughts, words, and actions—even (and especially) when it's hard—you cultivate self-control that honors him. This is a gift of the Holy Spirit!

As a believer, your identity in Christ means that God will never leave you nor forsake you (Hebrews 13:5). Consider the grace of God that you've received through the gospel. The Holy Spirit has given you a sound mind that is to be directed by the Scriptures. He enables you to be self-controlled rather than controlled by your own desires. Because of Christ, you can move *toward* God instead of away from him. As you behold his grace, the Spirit will equip you for the fight, and the fruit of self-control will grow.

> **Ask:** When did you last show self-control? How did the Holy Spirit help you? What factors make you more likely to give in to temptation or overindulgence?
>
> **Confess:** Father, forgive me for believing that when I lack self-control, I can simply try harder and produce the fruit of the Spirit by my own strength. Help me to rest in my identity in Christ and in your power to fill me with self-control.
>
> **Discover:** In Christ, I grow in self-control through the power of the Spirit, that I might continually draw near to God and walk in his ways.

I AM STEADFAST IN THE FAITH

And without faith it is impossible to please him, for whoever would draw near to God must believe that he exists and that he rewards those who seek him. (Hebrews 11:6)

Do you know any die-hard sports fans? They wear their favorite players' jerseys. They memorize all the stats. They are still reporting play-by-plays a week later. Their faithfulness makes sense when the team is playing well and winning games.

But I struggle to understand the dedication of these fans when their team is always losing. Or, worse, when its winning streak is the proven result of cheating.

Apart from Jesus, God's devotion to sinners is just as inexplicable.

As a Christian, have you ever worried that God is disappointed in you? Or that he's tired of supporting you? We want to believe that God is unswervingly committed to us, but we wonder if this could really be true. Does God remain faithful, even when we don't?

In Hebrews 11:6, we are told that without faith it is impossible for us to please God. But faith itself is a gift we receive from God (Ephesians 2:8). It's not our faithfulness that saves us; it's Christ's. By faith, we are saved from death because we believe in the finished work of our faithful Messiah. Now we are called to display the faithfulness of Christ through our thoughts, words, and actions.

Knowing your need, God gives you the Holy Spirit to faithfully fill your life with fruit—including the fruit of faithfulness (Galatians 5:22). The Spirit enables you to become what you are not on your own: increasingly faithful to God. He might help you to defend your faith when talking to friends who don't know Jesus. He might lead you to work in the church nursery or to tithe your money. The Holy Spirit can call you to respond to him with faithfulness in countless ways.

But remember, it's not your faithfulness that endears you to God! You are loved by God because Christ's faithfulness to God is credited to you. Jesus's perfect track record takes the place of your imperfect one. This means your faith in Jesus frees you from constantly laboring to prove your faithfulness to God. You have the incomprehensible and unwavering support of the Lord, by faith, for faith.

Christian, you are not defined by your successes, your failures, or the strength of your faith. You are loved and supported by God, who is more faithful to you than the most die-hard sports fan in the world. And now, because the Holy Spirit works within you, you are filled with his fruit so that you might live faithfully, proclaiming the good news that God is for you.

Ask: Are you tempted to measure God's love for you by the strength of your faith? Why is that unhelpful?

Confess: Father, I confess that I often attempt to be faithful through my own strength. Forgive me for trying to impress you, when I should rest in your promise to fill me with the fruit of faithfulness.

Discover: In Christ, I am filled with the fruit of the Spirit, empowered to live by faith and to joyfully reflect God's faithfulness to me, that all the world might see.

I AM STRENGTHENED TO ENDURE

*For if anyone is a hearer of the word and not a doer, he is like
a man who looks intently at his natural face in a mirror. For he
looks at himself and goes away and at once forgets what he
was like. But the one who looks into the perfect law, the law of
liberty, and perseveres, being no hearer who forgets but a doer
who acts, he will be blessed in his doing. (James 1:23–25)*

As Asher slurped his last spoonful of cereal, his mom asked him
to clean the kitchen. Dishes were his brother's chore, and he hadn't
made the mess. Asher began to scrape crusted eggs from plates
while his brother corrected his cleaning technique. Then his sis-
ter slinked in and dropped her dishes aggressively into the sink.
Breakfast remnants splashed onto his shirt.

Frustrated with everyone, Asher turned up the music on the
kitchen speaker in an effort to relax. But when his siblings started
making fun of his playlist, Asher snapped, lurched at his brother,
and punched him. When his mom grounded him, he yelled at
her too.

Hours later, Asher felt remorse for leaving the house that
morning without apologizing. He loved his family, and he hated
thinking about how he'd hurt them. As the Holy Spirit brought
James 1:23 to mind, he felt a twinge of conviction. He thought
about what Jesus had done for him, and he knew he needed God's
help not just to hear but to *do* God's Word.

As the family made dinner that evening, Asher apologized for
how he'd behaved at breakfast. His mom and his brother forgave
him—he knew they would. But then his mom hugged him and
asked, "Doesn't messing up make you see your need for Jesus so
clearly? Doesn't it make you so grateful for the gospel?"

James 1:23–25 serves as an identity check for Christians who've
forgotten their sin, their guilt, and their gracious salvation from

God's wrath. When we ignore our sin or fail to respond in obedience to God, we are like the person who looks in the mirror and forgets what he looks like.

Instead, James invites us to look into the perfect "law of liberty" without fear. As we read God's Word, we see our sin clearly. But we also see Christ, and as we discover the goodness of the gospel, we are reminded that he strengthens us. He blesses us and gives us his help in our "doing."

When you sense the Spirit's conviction as you face your sin, don't be afraid. This is a good sign that the Spirit is at work within you. Take the next step. Respond to your conviction. Maybe anger isn't your main struggle. Maybe you hope to put jealousy, pride, or lust to death. The Spirit provides countless opportunities to grow in Christlikeness.

You will need God's help to be a hearer and a doer of God's Word. Ask him to kill your sin and stir you to good works. He will fill you with fruit of the Spirit and make you more like Jesus.

Ask: When you sin, do you worry that God is angry with you? Does shame keep you from repentance or obedience? How would you be helped by seeing yourself in light of Christ's sacrifice for you?

Confess: Father, I confess that I don't always obey what I read in your Word. Help me to respond to your love by becoming both a hearer and a doer of the Word.

Discover: In Christ, I am a hearer and a doer who trusts in God's steadfast love.

CONCLUSION

Who are you? What is your purpose? How does who you are impact how you live?

Forget what you look like or how you dress. Forget how your school friends might describe you. Forget the sports you're good at or all the volunteer hours you've racked up for your college applications. And while you're at it, forget all of your mistakes too.

If you are in Christ, none of those things define you. When God looks at you, he only sees the righteousness, or right-standing, of Christ. Do you?

Discovering who you are in Christ frees you from the urge to construct your own identity and invites you to live confidently as who you are in Christ.

In Mark 10, Jesus meets a rich young man who is happy to tell him how amazing he's been his whole life, keeping all of God's commands. Kneeling before Jesus (and perhaps hoping for a pat on the back), he asks, "Good Teacher, what must I do to inherit eternal life?" (verse 17). His riches aren't enough. His good behavior isn't enough. He wants status too. He wants to impress the Son of God.

Now, Jesus doesn't put the guy on blast. He looks at the man, loves him, and instructs him to sell everything in order to come and follow him. He invites the man to live like a true disciple by laying down every competing desire.

Jesus taught that discipleship is costly. He warned his followers about how difficult it is for those who have wealth to enter the kingdom of God, but he also assured them that all things are possible with God.

What competing identity is Jesus asking you to lay down? Is he asking you to delete your social media account rather than find your identity in the number of followers you have? Is he allowing you to ride the bench for a few games to help you learn that your worth isn't found in how many points you score? What makes you feel like *yourself*, and how would you react if it disappeared today?

It might feel impossible to find your identity in Jesus instead of in the people you love and the things you've worked hard to achieve. If you cast aside the idols in your heart for his sake, you might lose friends, followers, or even the support of your family. Jesus didn't mince words regarding the suffering that Christians will endure (John 16:33). But being rich, popular, talented, athletic, trendy, or influential pales in comparison to walking with Christ and finding your identity in him.

When Peter worried about leaving everything behind in order to follow Jesus, our Lord assured him that those who have done so will receive a hundredfold both now and in the age to come (Matthew 19:27–29). If you are in Christ, he will reward you with far more than you've ever sacrificed.

Who are you?

You are God's creation, designed to worship him. Will you come to him through faith in his Son?

Who are you in Christ?

If you are in Christ, all that belongs to the Father is yours. You need not prove yourself. You need not earn his favor. You belong to Jesus, and he cares for you. You are part of the body of Christ.

Now you are led by the Holy Spirit. Your life has order, direction, and purpose, and you are called to good works. You are being made new, and the Spirit will cultivate his fruit within your heart as he conforms you to the image of Christ. You are strengthened by his life-giving promises.

How will you live, now that you know?

You are a new creation, filled by the Spirit of God, abounding in his fruit, reflecting the beauty of Jesus to everyone around you.

Discover who you are by walking with Jesus as a beloved disciple. He will remind you of your hope in the gospel. He will help you rest in his righteousness. He will lead you to good works that allow you to share in his riches both now and in eternity. As you follow Jesus, he will help you to understand *who you are*—and he will be praised and glorified through you.

ACKNOWLEDGMENTS

Psalm 27:13–14 says, "I believe that I shall look upon the goodness of the LORD in the land of the living! Wait for the LORD; be strong, and let your heart take courage; wait for the LORD!" God regularly reminds me of his goodness in this world by allowing me writing opportunities and solid friendships. Both fill me with courage to trust the Lord and to wait patiently on him, even when it feels exhausting or overwhelming.

Writing a book is never a small endeavor, but somehow I thought that writing a devotional might be simpler. It wasn't. And yet, it was the Lord's kind providence to set this project before me—he knew that I would need plenty of comfort during a particularly challenging season and that writing would provide countless opportunities to reconsider the good news of the gospel and to remember my identity in Jesus.

Thank you, Dave Almack, for inviting me to write this book even though I'd planned to take a breather from writing. Thank you, Chelsea Erickson and Amanda Martin, for the grace you showed me during the editing process and for helping my words make sense when upheaval and grief clouded my brain. Thank you, Megan Hill, for making sure I didn't give up on writing (or ministry) forever and for always praying. Thank you, Madeline, Allisa, Kari, Karen, Gretchen, Nancy, Reneé, Elizabeth, Sharon, Maria, Becky, Kim, and Judith—for your long-term friendship. Each of you has helped me to understand who I am in Christ by how you live out your faith.

And last, but certainly not least, thank you to the Carlson men. To my main man, Kyle: thank you for being the first to regularly teach and remind me who I am in Jesus. And thank you for sending me to the clubhouse, ensuring I had earbuds, and riding the writing roller coaster of emotions again. And to my boys-becoming-men, you guys are the GOATs. You are precious. Hilarious. Endless content creators. You never leave me lacking for stories and object lessons. I wrote this book because I love each of you and because, more than anything, I want you to embrace your identity in Christ.

Rooted Ministry's mission is to equip and empower churches and parents to faithfully disciple students toward lifelong faith in Jesus Christ. Our vision is to transform youth and family ministry so that every student receives grace-filled, gospel-centered and Bible-saturated discipleship in the church and at home.

Rooted was born in response to the crisis in the spiritual lives of young people. What started with a small conference has grown into a movement to see gospel-centered youth ministry become the normative experience of teenagers throughout the church. Rooted promotes gospel-centered youth ministry through books, conferences, curriculum and courses, articles, podcasts, mentorship, webinars, and more.

Rooted's 2021 release, *The Jesus I Wish I Knew in High School*, features stories from thirty authors about bullying, eating disorders, addiction, racism, family conflict, and the intense pressure to achieve, demonstrating how knowing Jesus brings rest and healing. In 2023, P&R Publishing and Rooted launched the 31-Day Devotional Series for Teenagers. The first book in the series, Liz Edrington's *Anxiety: Finding the Better Story*, won The Gospel Coalition's 2023 book award for devotional literature.

Rooted embraces a simple approach to youth ministry based on our understanding of Scripture and validated by research on effective models for cultivating sustainable faith in young people. We emphasize five pillars of youth ministry which include gospel centrality, theological depth through biblical teaching, relational discipleship, partnership with parents, and integration with the whole church body.

Rooted uses this framework to promote faithful discipleship of young people through the adults who love them. Imagine the impact on teenagers' lives if each week they are taught God's Word, prayed for, and mentored to understand God's grace for them through Christ. Rooted is reaching thousands of students by equipping their leaders for this type of meaningful ministry.

To learn more about Rooted, visit www.rootedministry.com.